D1714467

A Special Gift

Written and illustrated by Greg Armstrong

High in a tree, Kola the koala bear wakes up from her nap.

page 2

Kola looks up to see a bee. The bee says, "My name is Buddy. What is your name? "

page 4

Buddy sits on a branch and asks Kola, "Why are you so sad?"

page 6

Kola replies, "I want to be a Mommy."

page 8

Kola knocks on Buddy's door, louder and louder!

Kola hugs Buddy and tells
him she is going to be
a Mommy!

page 12

Mrs. Bee and Buddy are
very happy for Kola.

Buddy flies over to look
at Kola's baby.

page16

Buddy wants to know the
baby's name.

page 18

The baby was growing inside Kola's pouch, and he would be called, Snow.

Buddy peeked into Kola's
pouch and saw a little
white ball of fur.

All the birds made fun of Kola's baby because he looked different.

page 24

Soon all the animals in
the forest knew of the
new baby.

page 26

Buddy peeked into the pouch to find a frightened baby.

page 28

Snow grabbed Buddy's finger and soon they became friends.

page 30

Kola became sad because
Snow was getting so big.

page 32

Snow did not want to come out because he felt different.

page 34

Every day Buddy tried to
help Snow,
but Snow was too scared
to come out.

page 36

Buddy reminded Snow
how beautiful he was,
and to be proud of
his color.

page 38

Buddy brought Snow glasses to help him see the good in people.

page 40

Snow crawled out to see
the smile and love from
his mom.

page 42

Buddy and Snow walked
together, ignoring
everyone who was
pointing and
laughing at them.

page 44

Buddy took Snow to a
very special place his
mom used to take him.

page 46

Snow jumped on Buddy's
back. He saw animals
who were special,
like himself.

page 48

Snow turned to Buddy
and said, "I feel much
better now.
Thank you, Buddy."

page 50

Snow and Buddy walked
home as the best
of friends.

Snow was so happy. He started playing with all his new friends.

page 54

Regardless of Snow's
color, he was created
out of love.

We all were!

page 56

With one stroke of " His brush"...You became his

MASTERPIECE